EASIEST 5-FIN
PIANO COURSE

Complete with a repertoire of well-known songs to build your 5-finger skills!

Wise Publications
part of The Music Sales Group
London / New York / Paris / Sydney / Copenhagen / Berlin / Madrid / Tokyo

Introduction

Welcome to the Easiest 5-Finger Piano Course...

Playing the piano is amazingly rewarding and with this book, you'll discover that *learning* to play can be great fun as well!

Whether this is the first time you've ever played a musical instrument or you are using this course as a refresher, you'll find that the simple explanations, well-known songs and step-by-step approach used in this book help to make learning more enjoyable. This approach will get you playing the piano from the first time you sit at the keyboard, and you'll be reading music in very little time.

This book is equally suitable if you are teaching yourself to play, or you have a teacher to guide you through the course.

The 5-finger technique employs a fixed position for your hands for each piece of music you play — each finger is assigned to one particular note of the piano keyboard. This is perfect for beginners as it makes the learning process simpler to start with and can yield faster results.

The course is divided into eight lessons and at the back of the book you'll find seven songs and tunes, bringing together all your new techniques and starting your list of performance repertoire!

It is not intended that you should necessarily work through a whole lesson in one go — you can take the course at whatever pace suits you. This might be a page or a two-page spread at a time. The key to learning the piano well and improving fast is practice. It is good to repeat the songs and exercises a number of times, so that you become confident with all the new techniques you are learning. Each time you sit down to play, it is useful to recap what you've already learnt, by playing through some music from a previous lesson. It's true that 'practice makes perfect', and you'll find that having short but regular practice sessions is much more valuable than for example, a long, concentrated session once a week.

By the end of the course, you will have mastered the technique of playing using the 5-finger approach and reading music, and you'll be ready to explore all the repertoire books in the **Easiest 5-Finger Piano Collection**.

I hope you have many hours of fun with this book and that you get lots of enjoyment from your piano playing. And with any luck, by the end of this course, you will be such a master of the piano keyboard that others will enjoy your playing too!

Christopher Hussey

Contents

Lesson 1

Getting ready to play

Let's begin by finding a good playing position. Sit in front of your piano, facing the middle of the keyboard. Make sure that you are sitting a comfortable distance from the keyboard—not too close and not too far.

Try to keep a straight back, and keep your arms relaxed. Bring your hands up to the level of the keyboard and rest your fingertips lightly on the piano keys, placing each finger on a different white note.

Your forearms should be almost parallel to the floor (not at an angle) and they should sit level with the keyboard. Adjust the height of your seat, if you can, to achieve this.

Now, let's have a look at the layout of the piano keyboard. There are lots and lots of notes on your keyboard—if you're sitting at a full size piano, there are probably 88 of them!

Can you see any repeated patterns in the layout of the keys?

Notice that the black keys are arranged alternately in groups of two and three. In fact, the keyboard is made up of a series of 12 notes (five black keys and seven white keys) that repeat for the entire length of the piano.

The white keys in the series are given the letter names: **A B C D E F G**

To find the note **A**, look for a group of three black notes. **A** is the white note that sits between the 2nd and 3rd black note in the group of three.

Middle C

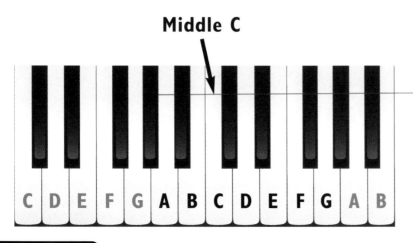

The note **C** that is nearest the middle of the piano is quite helpfully called **Middle C**.

Can you find this note?

(*Handy hint:* Look for the group of two black keys nearest the middle. **Middle C** is the white note just to the left of these.)

Positioning your right hand

The fingers of your right hand are numbered like this:

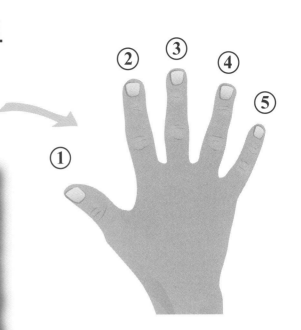

You can play a little game to become more familiar with these finger numbers.

Place your right hand palm down on a table top. Then, ask someone to slowly call out numbers between one and five. As each number is called, tap the finger it refers to.

Now let's put your right-hand fingers in their first fixed position.

Place your thumb ① on **Middle C**.

Now put your index finger ② on the white note above Middle C—**D**.

Then put your middle finger ③ on the next white note, **E**.

Put your ring finger ④ on the next white note, **F**.

...And finally, place your little finger ⑤ on the next white note, **G**.

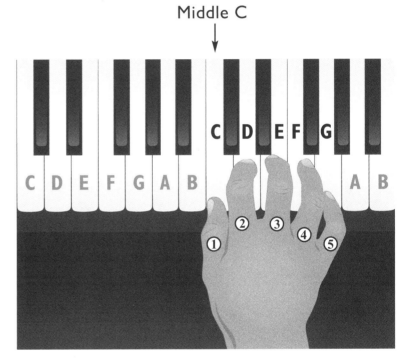

The position of your right hand can be shown in a diagram like this:

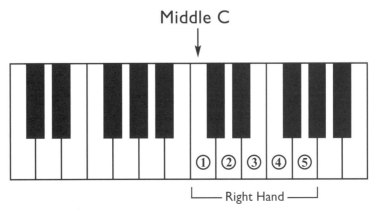

First notes

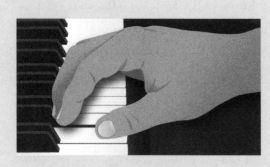

Hand shape and position

Your hand should be cupped, as if you were holding a small ball.

Your fingers should be nicely curved, with your fingertips (not your nails) lightly touching the keys, ready to play.

Your hand should be supported from your wrist, keeping your wrist and forearm up. Your wrist should be at the same level as your knuckles—don't let it drop below the level of the keyboard.

Try playing the sequence of notes below.

③ ② ① ③ ② ① ⑤ ④④ ③ ⑤ ④④ ③

Now, try playing this sequence with the correct rhythm, using the words to help you—you can sing them aloud or in your head as you play.

③ ② ① ③ ② ① ⑤ ④④ ③ ⑤ ④④ ③

Three blind mice, three blind mice. See how they run, see how they run!

Music is divided into **bars** by **barlines**.

barlines

final barline

bar ← → bar ← → bar ← → bar

A **final barline** marks the end of the music.

In 'Three Blind Mice' there are four beats in every bar. Try counting the beats aloud, keeping a steady four in each bar for four bars.

Count: 1 2 3 4 | 1 2 3 4 | 1 2 3 4 | 1 2 3 4 ‖

Say "1 – 2 – 3 – 4, 1 – 2 – 3 – 4, 1 – 2 – 3 – 4, 1 – 2 – 3 – 4."

Keeping time

Play the tune again, this time counting the beats out loud, keeping a steady rhythm as you play.

Count:	1 2 3 4	1 2 3 4	1 2 3 4	1 2 3 4 ‖
R.H.	③ ② ①	③ ② ①	⑤ ④④③	⑤ ④④③
	Three blind mice,	three blind mice.	See how they run,	see how they run!

R.H. stands for Right Hand—in this row, you'll see what finger pattern to play.

Now, let's try some more phrases from well-known songs. Sing the words aloud (or in your head) as you play to help you with the rhythm.

Count:	1 2 3 4	1 2 3 4	1 2 3 4	1 2 3 4 ‖
R.H.	① ② ③ ①	① ② ③ ①	③ ④ ⑤	③ ④ ⑤
	Frè - re Jac - ques,	Frè - re Jac - ques,	dor - mez - vous?	Dor - mez - vous?

Count:	1 2 3 4	1 2 3 4	1 2 3 4	1 2 3 4
R.H.	③ ② ① ②	③ ③ ③	② ② ②	③ ⑤ ⑤
	Mer - ri - ly we	roll a - long,	roll a - long,	roll a - long.

Count:	1 2 3 4	1 2 3 4	1 2 3 4	1 2 3 4 ‖
R.H.	③ ② ① ②	③ ③ ③	② ② ③ ②	①
	Mer - ri - ly we	roll a - long,	o'er the deep blue	sea.

Count:	1 2 3 4	1 2 3 4	1 2 3 4	1 2 3 4
R.H.	③ ③ ③	③ ③ ③	③ ⑤ ① ②	③
	Jin - gle bells,	jin - gle bells,	jin - gle all the	way.

Count:	1 2 3 4	1 2 3 4	1 2 3 4	1 2 3 4 ‖
R.H.	④ ④ ④ ④	④ ③ ③ ③③	⑤ ⑤ ④ ②	①
	Oh, what fun it	is to ride in a	one-horse o - pen	sleigh!

Now try playing the phrases above whilst counting a steady four beats to a bar.

Lesson 2

Positioning your left hand

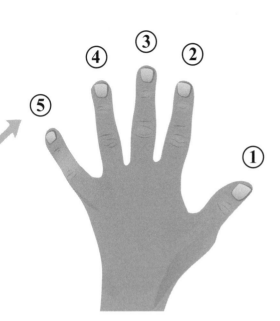

The fingers of your left hand are numbered like this...

To become more familiar with these finger numbers, play the game you learnt on page 5, where someone calls out finger numbers between one and five and you tap the corresponding finger on a table.

Let's position your left hand now in its first fixed position. Start by placing your thumb ① on the note **B** just below *Middle C*. You'll find this note just to the left of *Middle C*.

Middle C

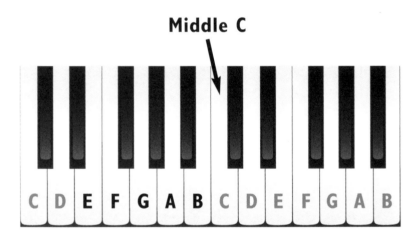

Now put your index finger ② on the next white note down, **A**.

Place your middle finger ③ on the next white note down, **G**.

Then put your ring finger ④ on **F**.

And finally, place your little finger ⑤ on **E**.

The position of your left hand can be shown in a diagram like this:

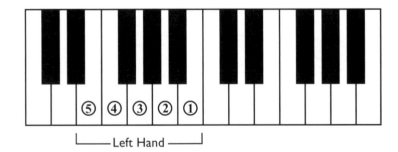

Check your left hand is in a comfortable and suitable position to play, supported by your wrist and with curved fingers (see page 6).

In the following exercises, **L.H.** stands for Left Hand — in this row, you'll see what finger pattern to play in your left hand.

Some left-hand finger patterns...

Practise the pattern of the phrase below — slowly to begin with, and don't worry about the rhythm yet.

Count: 1 2 3 4 | 1 2 3 4 | 1 2 3 4 | 1 2 3 4 |
L.H. ⑤ ④ ③ | ④ ③ ② | ③ ② ① ③ | ⑤ ④ ③ |

Count: 1 2 3 4 | 1 2 3 4 | 1 2 3 4 | 1 2 3 4 ‖
L.H. ⑤ ④ ③ ⑤ | ④ ③ ② ④ | ③ ② ① ③ | ⑤ ‖

Once you are familiar with the finger pattern, count the beats aloud and try to play it with the correct rhythm.

Note that the next phrase starts on beat 4 of the first bar. Count "1 – 2 – 3" before starting to play. Sing the words aloud or in your head as you play, to help you with the rhythm.

Count: 1 2 3 4 | 1 2 3 4 | 1 2 3 4 | 1 2 3 4 |
L.H.   ③ | ③   ⑤ ② | ③   ⑤ ⑤ | ③ ③ ⑤ ② |
             A - tis - ket, a - tas - ket, a   green and yel - low

Count: 1 2 3 4 ‖
L.H. ③   ⑤ ‖
      bas - ket...

Now try playing the tune and counting the beats in each bar out loud. Keep the rhythm steady.

Here's another left-hand phrase that begins on beat 4 of the first bar.

Count: 1 2 3 4 | 1 2 3 4 | 1 2 3 4 ‖
L.H.   ③ ④ | ⑤ ③ ③ ③ | ② ③ ‖
          There's a   yel - low rose in   Tex - as...

Lesson 3

Putting your hands together

Place your right-hand fingers on the white notes in the position you have learnt. Start by placing your thumb on **Middle C** (*Handy hint:* Look on page 5 for a reminder).

Then, place your left hand in the position you learnt on page 8. Start by placing your LH thumb ① on the **B** just below *Middle C.*

Your hands are now positioned on the notes shown opposite, and you're ready to play hands together.

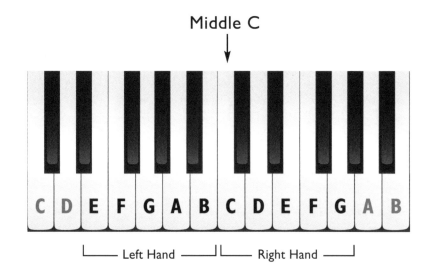

Here's a diagram that shows this fixed position for your left and right hands.

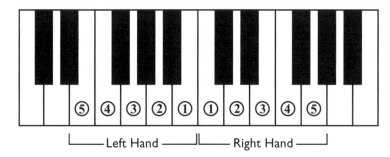

Try playing the following tune, singing the words aloud or in your head as you play.

This tune is mainly in your RH, but uses one finger of your LH every so often— ③. Which note is that?

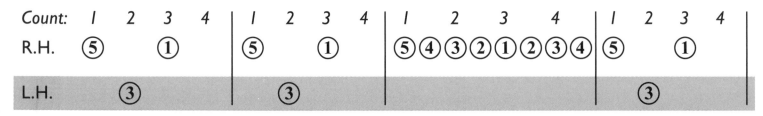

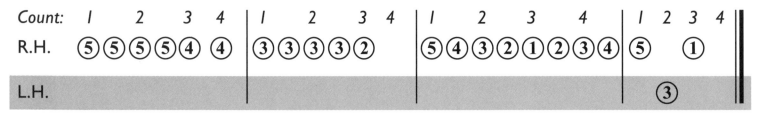

Play the next song very slowly to begin with, as you learn the finger pattern and practise changing between your RH and LH. Then, gradually increase the speed as you improve.

Note that this song starts on beat 3 of the first bar, so count "1 – 2" before you start to play.

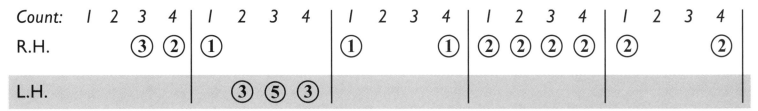

Oh, the grand old Duke of York, he had ten thou-sand men, he

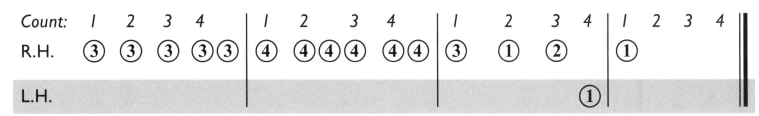

marched them up to the top of the hill and he marched them down a - gain!

Now, let's learn the finger pattern for 'Bobby Shafto'. Before playing, make sure your fingers are placed lightly on the correct notes ready to play, and that you have a nice hand shape, with curved fingers.

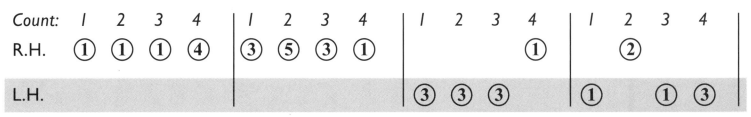

Bob - by Shaf - to's gone to sea,_____ sil - ver buck - les on his knee.___

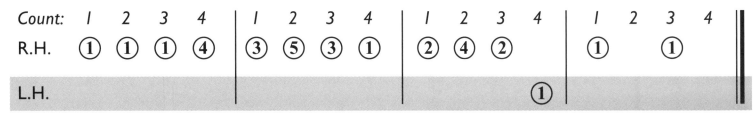

He'll come back and mar - ry me,_____ bon - ny Bob - by Shaf - to.

Once you are confident with the rhythm, count a steady four beats in every bar out loud as you play.

Play it through a number of times so you get to know the finger pattern well — we're going to use this song again on the next page.

Reading rhythm

Musical notation shows us the **rhythm** and **pitch** of a tune. Different types of notes are used, each with a different *note value* telling us how long they last.

♩ is called a **crotchet** (or **quarter note**)—it lasts one beat.

It can also be written like this: ♩

♩ is called a **minim** (or **half note**)—it lasts two beats.

It can also be written like this: ♩

A sequence of note values gives us the *rhythm* of the music.

The rhythm for 'Bobby Shafto' is very simple. Look back at page 11 and you'll see that every note is a **crotchet** (lasting for one beat) apart from the last two notes, which are **minims** (lasting for two beats each). So, the rhythm of the song can be written like this:

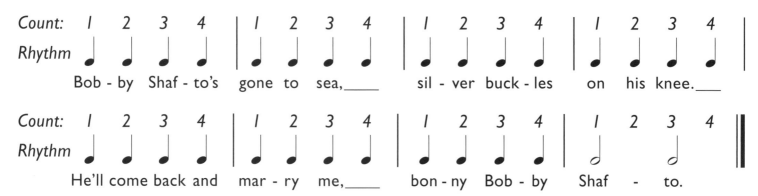

Count: 1 2 3 4 | 1 2 3 4 | 1 2 3 4 | 1 2 3 4 |

Rhythm ♩ ♩ ♩ ♩ | ♩ ♩ ♩ ♩ | ♩ ♩ ♩ ♩ | ♩ ♩ ♩ ♩ |

Bob - by Shaf - to's gone to sea,____ sil - ver buck - les on his knee.___

Count: 1 2 3 4 | 1 2 3 4 | 1 2 3 4 | 1 2 3 4 ‖

Rhythm ♩ ♩ ♩ ♩ | ♩ ♩ ♩ ♩ | ♩ ♩ ♩ ♩ | ♩ ♩ ‖

He'll come back and mar - ry me,____ bon - ny Bob - by Shaf - to.

Reading the note values above, use one finger to tap out the rhythm of the tune on a table top.

Play 'Bobby Shafto' again, this time using the note values to show you the rhythm rather than the words. The finger number is given in a circle above each note.

Count: 1   2   3   4 | 1   2   3   4 | 1   2   3   4 | 1   2   3   4 |
        ①   ①   ①   ④   ③   ⑤   ③   ①   ①   ②
R.H.   ♩   ♩   ♩   ♩ | ♩   ♩   ♩   ♩ | ♩ | ♩ |
                                                 ③   ③   ③   ①   ①   ③
L.H.   ♩   ♩   ♩ | ♩ | ♩   ♩ |

Count: 1   2   3   4 | 1   2   3   4 | 1   2   3   4 | 1   2   3   4   ‖
        ①   ①   ①   ④   ③   ⑤   ③   ①   ②   ④   ②   ①   ①
R.H.   ♩   ♩   ♩   ♩ | ♩   ♩   ♩   ♩ | ♩   ♩   ♩ | ♩   ♩   ‖
                                                              ①
L.H.   ♩

Time signatures

4/4 This is called a **time signature**. It's written at the beginning of a piece of music to show you how many beats there are in each bar.

The top number shows you that there are four beats in each bar.

The bottom number tells us that each beat is a crotchet. So, this *time signature* tells us that there are *four crotchet beats in each bar*.

Always look carefully at the top number to see how many crotchet beats there are in each bar.

For example, **3/4** tells us there are *three crotchet beats in each bar,* and

2/4 tells us there are *two crotchet beats in each bar.*

The next phrase is just for your right hand, so put your fingers in place ready to play.

Use the note values to read the rhythm.

Do you recognise the song? *(Have a look at page 7.)*

o is called a **semibreve** (or **whole note**) — it lasts for four beats.

Still using just your RH, try the song below. Read the note values carefully and count a steady four beats in a bar as you play — practise slowly to begin with.

(Handy hint: If it helps, you can write the counts above the music.)

Lesson 4

Reading pitch

As well as showing us the *rhythm* of a tune, musical notation shows us which note to play, for example, whether to play a *C* or a *D*. This is called the **pitch** of a note.

A **stave** is made up of five lines. The *pitch* of a note is shown by its position on the *stave*.

A different pitch is written on every line and in every space of the stave.

The curly symbol at the start is called a **treble clef**, or 'g clef'—because it spirals around the line on which the note **G** just above *Middle C* is written. Also, the lower part of the clef looks a bit like a *g*.

The notes played by your right hand are written in the *treble clef*.

This is how you write **Middle C** in the *treble clef:*

Here's how you write the notes played by your right hand:

...And the notes continue going up the stave on every line and in every space.

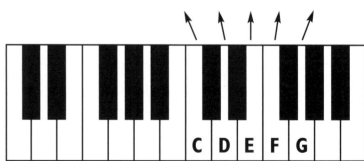

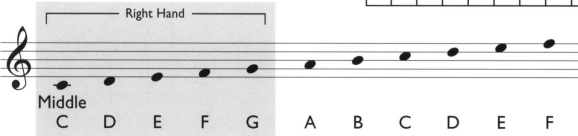

The stave is a bit like a ladder, and the lines and spaces are like the rungs—as you climb up the stave step-by-step, you are moving up the white notes of the piano.

With your right hand in position, try this familiar phrase. Don't worry about the rhythm to begin with, whilst you familiarise yourself with reading the changes of pitch.

The finger numbers are written above the music to help you.

When you are ready, count a steady and slow four in a bar and play the tune, reading the rhythm as well. Do you recognise this tune? *(Have a look at page 7.)*

Now try the tune below. Again, familiarise yourself with the finger pattern first of all, before you tackle playing in time. Try reading the music using the position of the notes on the stave to tell you which notes to play—the finger numbers are there to help you if you get stuck.

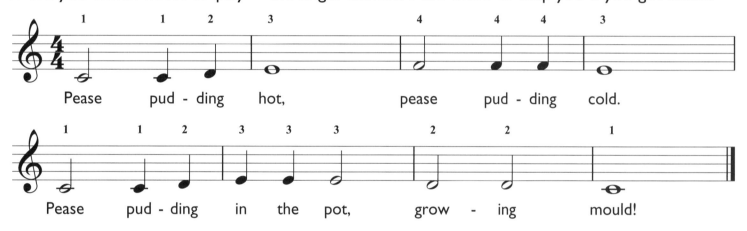

A **tie** joins two notes of the same pitch. Only the first note is played, and held for the length of both *tied* notes.

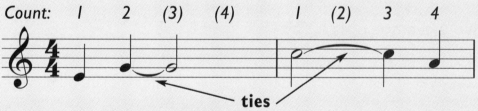

Watch out for the *ties* in the next song. The pitches don't change as often in this tune, so try reading the music slowly with the correct rhythm from the start.

15

And now for your left hand...

The notes played by your left hand are written on a *stave* in the **bass clef**.

This clef is also called the 'f clef', because the line between the two dots is the line on which the note **F** just below *Middle C* is written.

Also, if you were to draw a little horizontal line joining each of the dots to the curly symbol, the bass clef sign would look a bit like a capital *F*.

This is how you write **Middle C** in the *bass clef*:

This is how you write the notes played by your left hand:

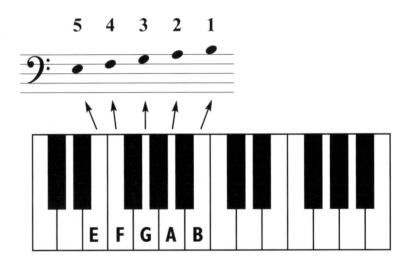

...And just like in the *treble clef*, the notes continue up and down the stave in the *bass clef*, with a note on every line and in every space.

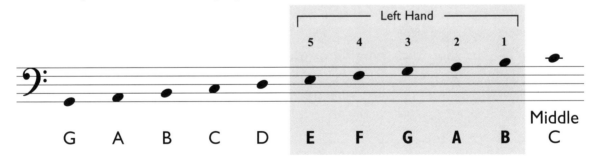

Try this simple left-hand tune. Work out the finger pattern first of all, as you become familiar with reading pitches in the *bass clef*. Then, count steadily and play the tune with its rhythm.

Reading both hands

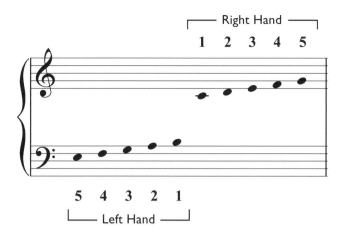

Piano music is written on a **grand stave**.

This consists of an upper stave headed by the *treble clef* and a lower stave headed by the *bass clef*.

The two staves are joined together, with a curly **brace** at the start of each line.

The *grand stave* above shows the position you've learnt for both hands.

Using the 5-finger method, the music in the *treble clef* is played by your right hand and the music in the *bass clef* is played by your left hand.

Try to play with your hands together now—count a steady four beats to the bar as you play.

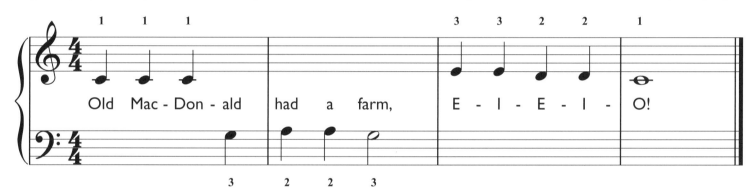

Now try this opening phrase from a well-known Christmas carol. Watch out, there is only one crotchet beat at the start—it is not a full bar of four beats. This shows you that the tune starts on beat 4 of the bar, so count "1 – 2 – 3" before you start to play.

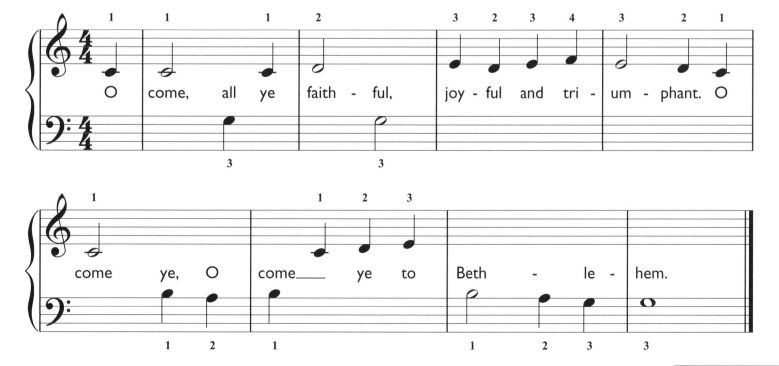

Lesson 5

A new position for your hands

Here's a fingering diagram and stave notation showing you a new position for your left and right hands.

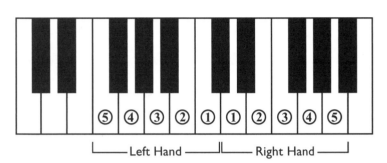

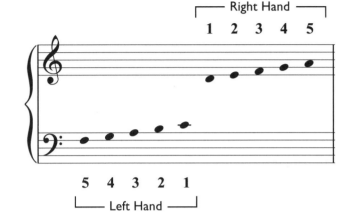

Start by positioning your right hand.

Put your RH thumb ① on the note **D** just above *Middle C*.

Then, put your RH index finger ② on the next white note up, **E**.

Continue, by placing your RH fingers ③ on **F**, ④ on **G** and ⑤ on **A**.

Now, keeping your RH fingers in position, place the fingers of your left hand, starting by putting your LH thumb ① on **Middle C**. Then, place your LH index finger ② on the next white note down, **B**. Continue, by placing your LH fingers ③ on **A**, ④ on **G** and ⑤ on **F**.

Make sure both your hands are in a good playing position, with level wrists and curved fingers, then try the tune below.

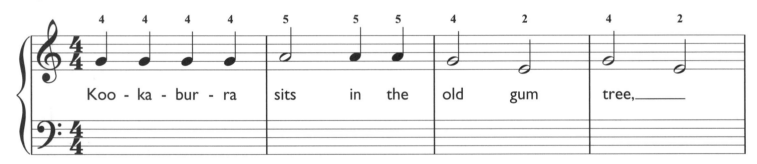

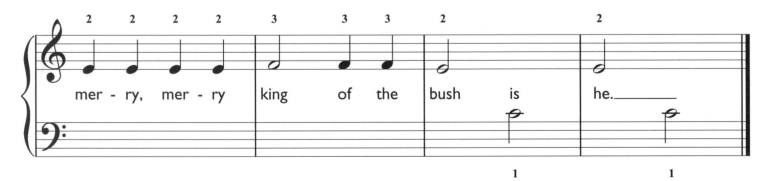

Once you have mastered the rhythm and notes to play, this tune should be played quite fast.

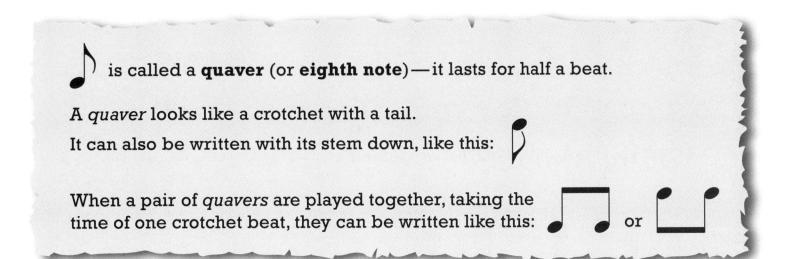

is called a **quaver** (or **eighth note**)—it lasts for half a beat.

A *quaver* looks like a crotchet with a tail.

It can also be written with its stem down, like this:

When a pair of *quavers* are played together, taking the time of one crotchet beat, they can be written like this: or

Make sure your fingers are placed in the new hand position shown opposite. Check that your wrists and fingers are in a good playing position, then try the next song.

Count four beats in every bar in your head, keeping a steady beat, and watch out for the *quavers*—some have separate tails and some pairs are joined together.

THIS OLD MAN

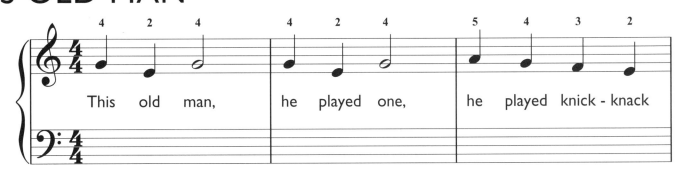

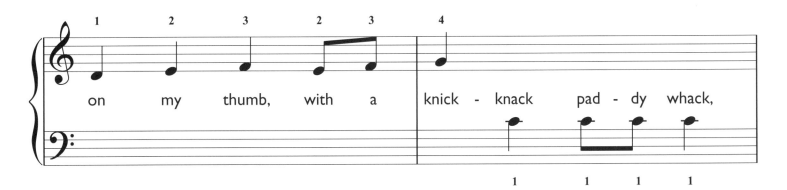

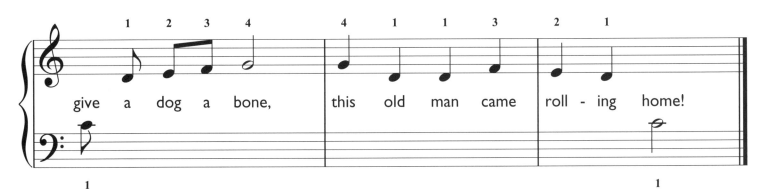

Place your hands in the new position you have just learnt (page 18), then try the next song.

Watch out for the *ties* (see page 15)—remember, hold tied notes for the length of both notes and don't play the second note.

Count a steady four beats a bar in your head to help you get the rhythm right.

LONDON BRIDGE

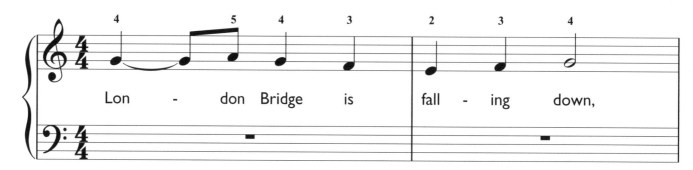

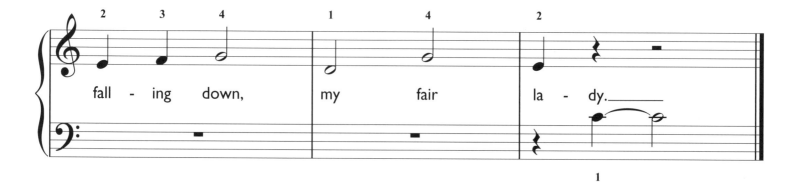

Did you notice that there are some new symbols used in this song?

These are called **rests**. A rest is used instead of a note to tell you to be silent. (For example, you'll see rests in the RH when the LH takes over the tune.)

is a *crotchet rest,* which tells you to be silent for a crotchet—one beat.

is a *minim rest,* which tells you to be silent for a minim—two beats.

is a *semibreve rest,* which tells you to be silent for a semibreve—four beats.

Flats, sharps and key signatures

We use **flats** and **sharps** to describe the black notes on the piano.

A sharp sign ♯ raises a note by one step to the very next key on the right. So, for example, F becomes **F♯** (F sharp).

The **F♯** above *Middle C* is written like this:

F♯
(F sharp)

A flat sign ♭ lowers a note by one step to the very next key on the left. So, for example, B becomes **B♭** (B flat).

The **B♭** above *Middle C* is written like this:

B♭
(B flat)

Try finding some other *flat* and *sharp* notes: E♭ *(E flat)*, A♭ *(A flat)*, C♯ *(C sharp)*, G♯ *(G sharp)*.

Notice that A♭ and G♯ are two names for the same note. All black notes can be described as either *flats* or *sharps*, depending on whether you go down a step or up a step from a white note.

Key signatures

In the key of **F major**, all Bs are *flat*. This can be shown by a **key signature**.

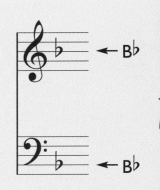

A *key signature* is written at the start of each line of music. It tells us which notes should be played as either *flats* or *sharps*, and saves writing a ♭ or ♯ sign every time those notes appear.

This *key signature* shows a ♭ on the line on which Bs are written in both clefs. Every time you read a B, you should play a B♭ (B flat).

A hand position in F major

Find this new hand position, which uses a B♭ in your left hand, then try the next song.

(*Handy hint:* This hand position is like the one you learnt on page 18, except your LH index finger ② is on B♭, rather than B).

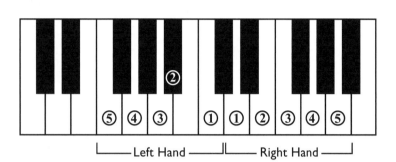

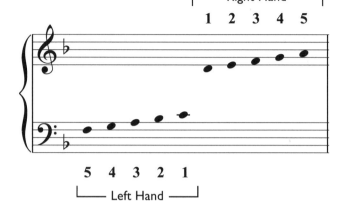

The **key signature** used here shows you that all Bs should be played as B♭s (B flats). You can write the flat sign in before each B if it helps you remember.

BAA, BAA, BLACK SHEEP

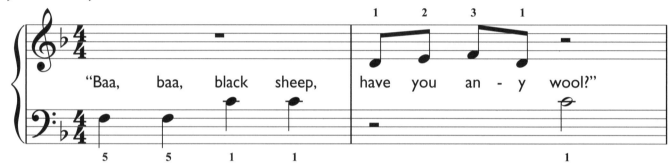

♪ is a *quaver rest,* which tells you to be silent for a quaver — half a beat.

Dotted notes and rhythms

A **dot** after a note tells you to increase the length of the note by half of its normal value.

♩. is a **dotted crotchet**—it lasts for one and a half beats: ♩. = ♩ + ♪

♩. is a **dotted minim**—it lasts for three beats: ♩. = ♩ + ♩

Before you play the next song, make sure you're comfortable playing these dotted rhythms.

Counts 1 2 3 4   *1 2 3 4*

This rhythm...   ...can be written like this:

Counts 1 2 + 3 4   *1 2 + 3 4*

This rhythm...   ...can be written like this:

CAMPTOWN RACES

The Camp - town la - dies sing this song,

doo - dah, doo - dah! Camp - town race - track's

five miles long, oh, de - doo - dah - day!

Lesson 7

A new key and a new hand position

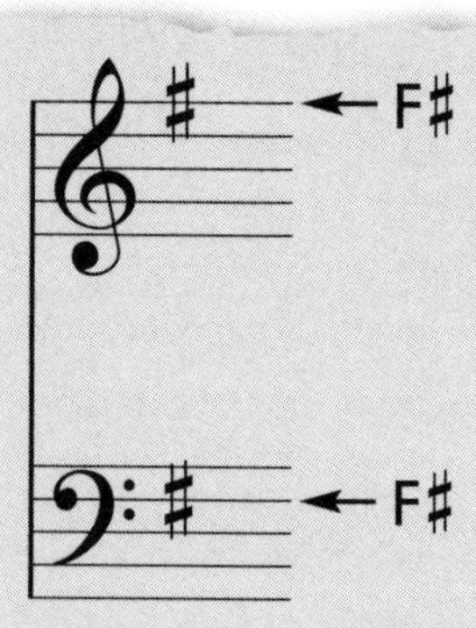

This is the *key signature* for **G major**. It tells us that all Fs are to be played as F♯s (F sharps).

Can you find the first F♯ above *Middle C*? Start by finding F, then raise it one step to the black note on the right—this is **F♯**.

Can you find the F♯ below that one?

Here's your new hand position in G major.

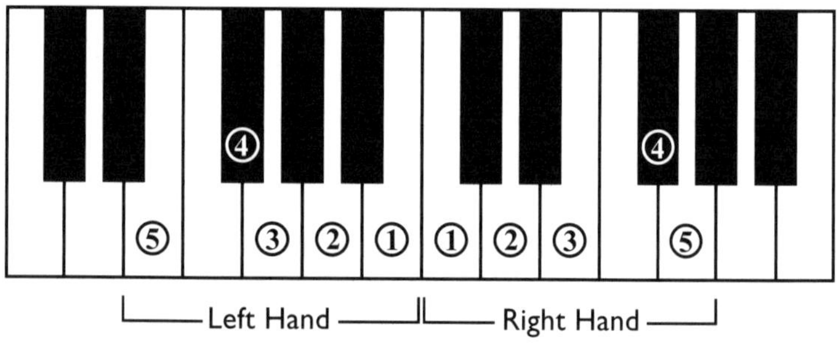

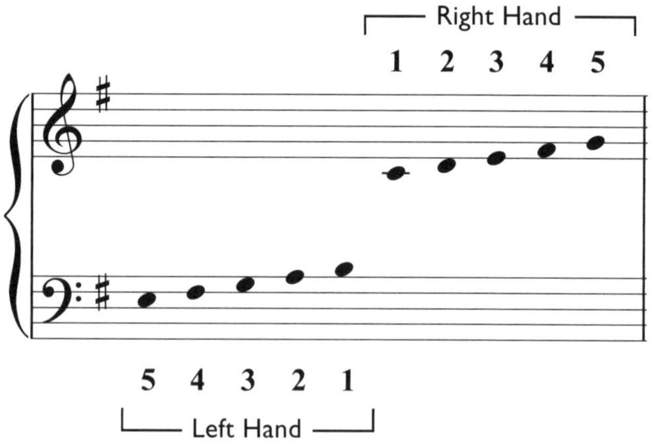

Notice that this position is very similar to the first hand position you learnt (RH on page 5 and LH on page 8), except that the Fs are F♯s this time. The easiest way to find this new position is to put all your fingers in the first position you learnt (all on the white keys), and then raise your ring finger ④ in both hands up a step, from F to **F♯**.

3/4 The next tune is from a piece of music by Johann Sebastian Bach. Have a look at the time signature. It tells us that there are three crotchet beats in every bar.

So, you should count "1 – 2 – 3, 1 – 2 – 3" *etc.* out loud or in your head. (*Handy hint:* It might help you to write the counts above the music or between the staves.)

Notice that the semibreve rest 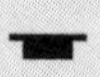 is also used to show a full bar's rest in the 'Minuet', even though there are only three beats in each bar.

This rest can be used to show a full bar's rest in *any* time signature.

MINUET IN G

Don't forget that the *key signature* tells us that all Fs are to be played as F♯s.

Lesson 8

A new position in the key of C major

This is the *key signature* for **C major**.

It tells us that there are no flats or sharps in the music, so it is played only on the white keys of the piano.

The first two positions you learnt for your left and right hands were also in C major—can you remember them?

Now find the new position for your hands shown below. Notice that your thumbs both share the note **D**—sometimes the *D* will be played by your RH and sometimes by your LH.

Place the fingers of your right hand first, beginning with your RH thumb ① , and then place the fingers of your left hand, beginning with your LH thumb ① .

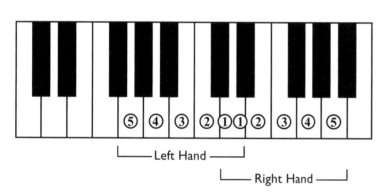

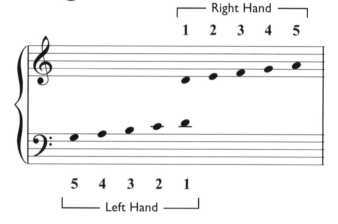

LAVENDER'S BLUE

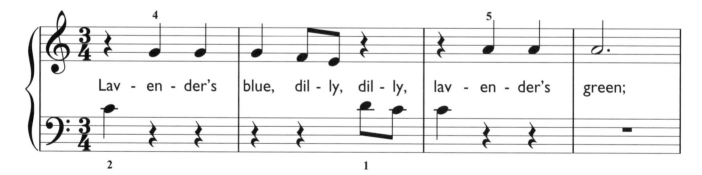

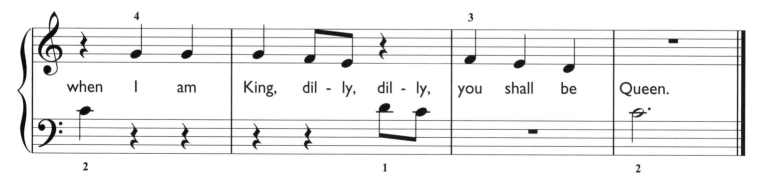

There are no longer finger numbers above every note—just at certain points, to help you.

The next song uses the same hand position. Take a look at the time signature before you begin to play. Notice that this song starts on beat 4 of the bar and begins with a quaver rest, so count "1 – 2 – 3 – 4" before playing the first note.

The last four bars include an accompaniment in your left hand. Practise these bars hands separately to begin with, and then put them together, slowly at first.

A-TISKET, A-TASKET

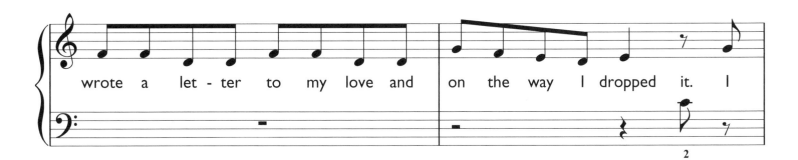

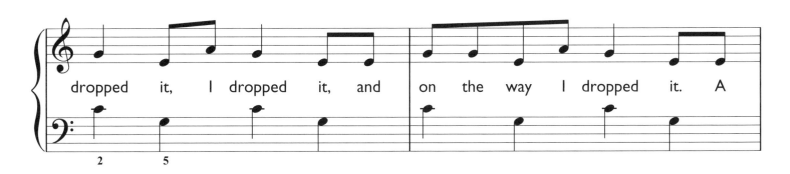

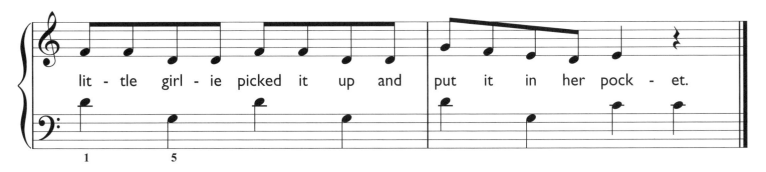

Notice that four quavers in a row can be joined together, like in the second full bar ("green and yellow").

Well done! You've completed the Easiest 5-Finger Piano Course now and you're ready to play the selection of songs over the next few pages, using the positions you've learnt.

On the last page of this book, you'll find details of lots more books in the series for you to enjoy. All the songs and tunes in the collection use the Easiest 5-Finger Piano approach, and now you know everything you need to enjoy playing your way through them! Happy piano playing!

TWINKLE, TWINKLE, LITTLE STAR

Traditional

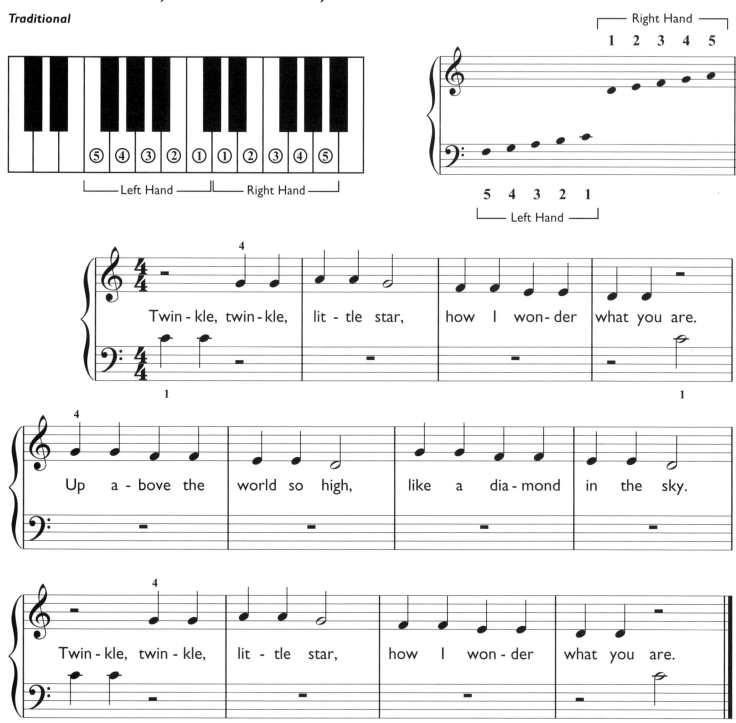

POLLY PUT THE KETTLE ON

Traditional

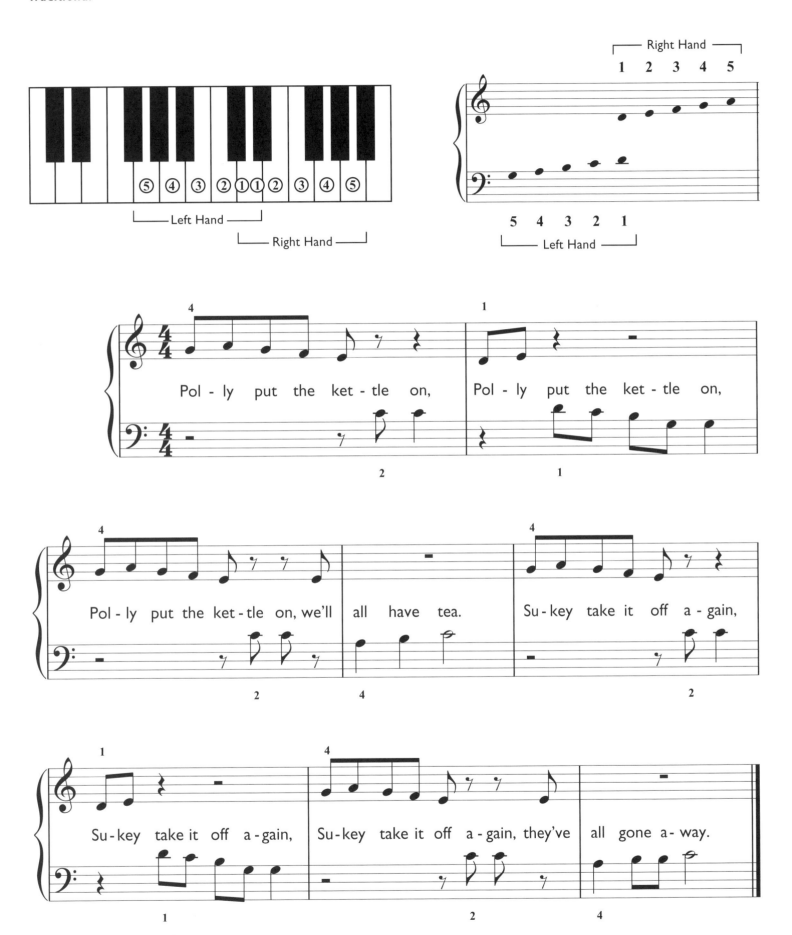

AWAY IN A MANGER

Traditional

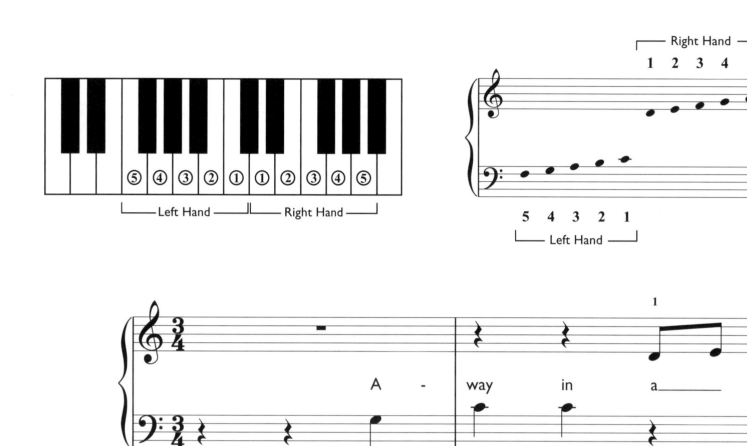

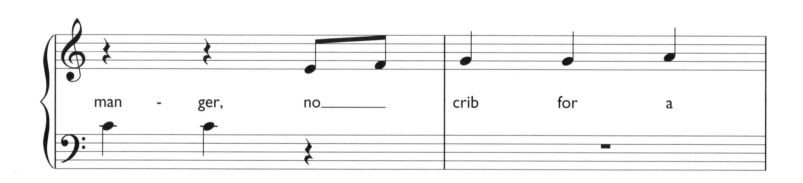

A - way in a man - ger, no____ crib for a

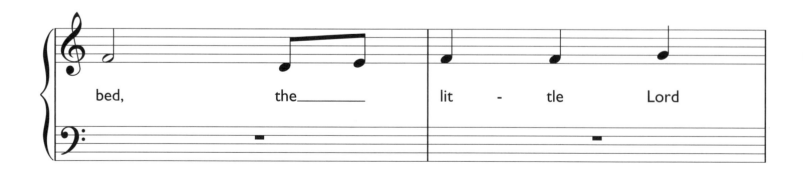

bed, the____ lit - tle Lord

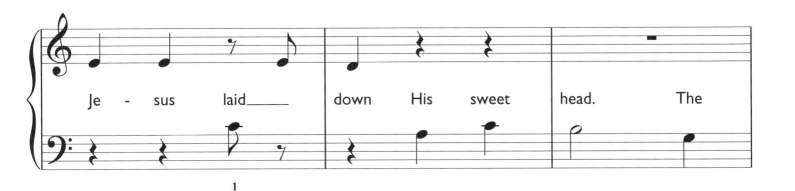

Je - sus laid_____ down His sweet head. The

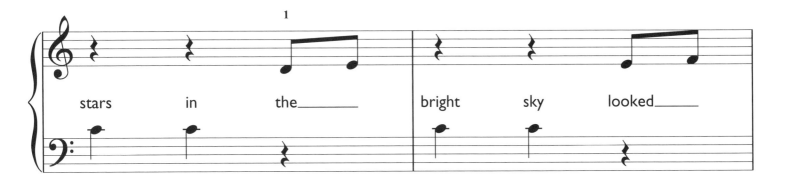

stars in the_____ bright sky looked_____

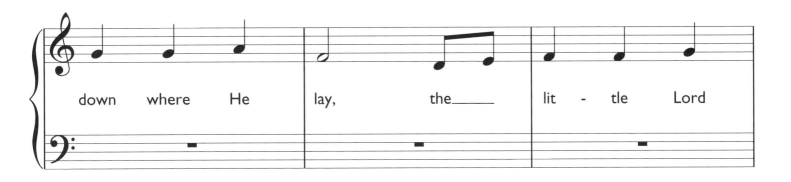

down where He lay, the_____ lit - tle Lord

Je - sus, a - sleep on the hay.

SPRING (from 'The Four Seasons')

Composed by Antonio Vivaldi

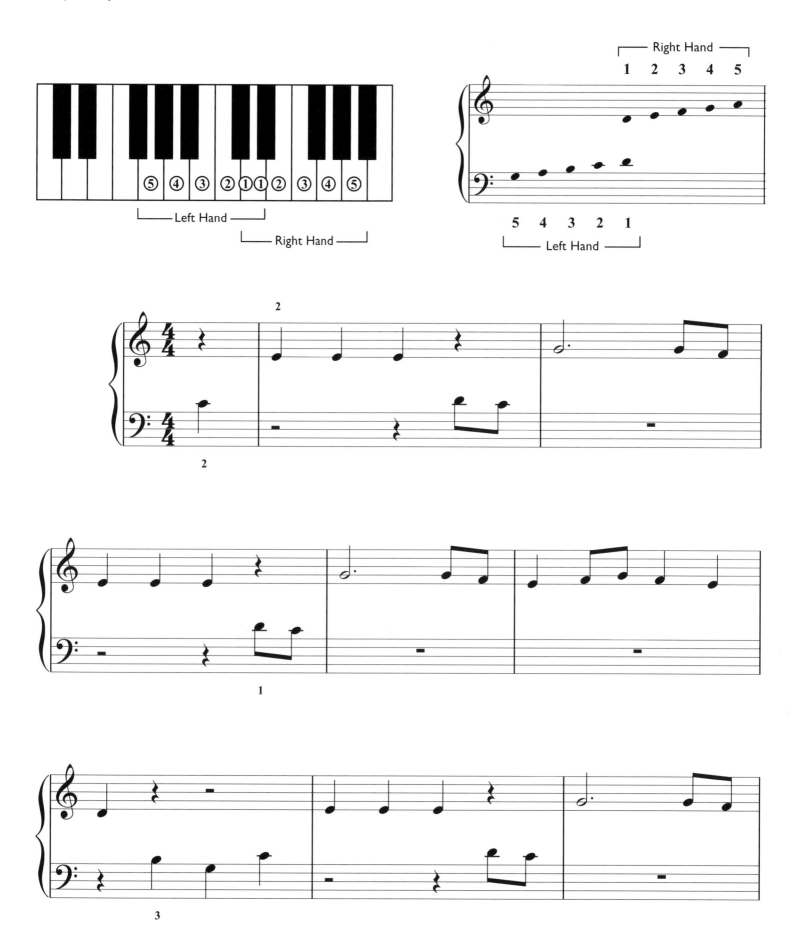

OLD MACDONALD HAD A FARM

Traditional

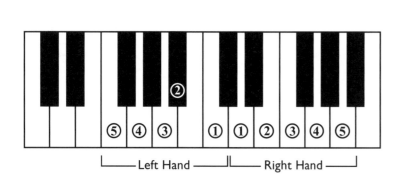

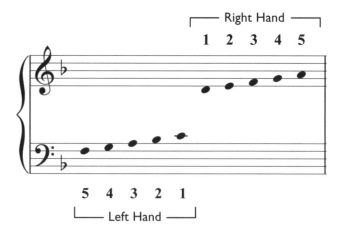

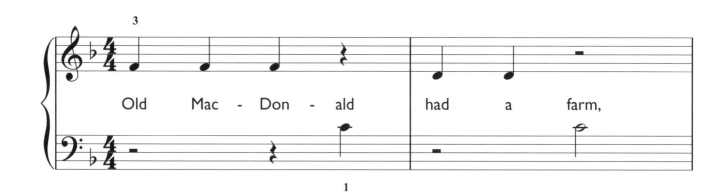

Old   Mac - Don - ald   had   a   farm,

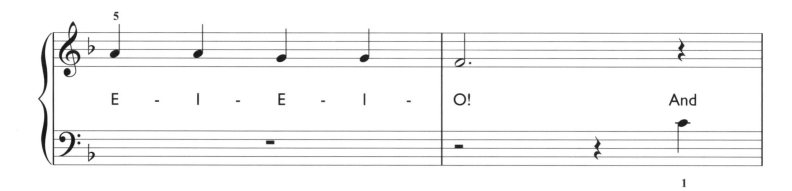

E - I - E - I - O!   And

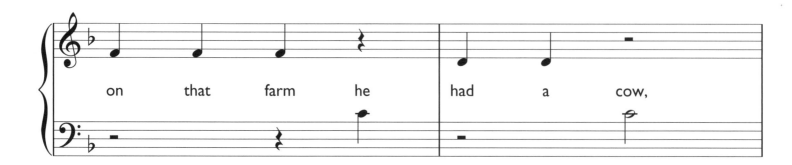

on   that   farm   he   had   a   cow,

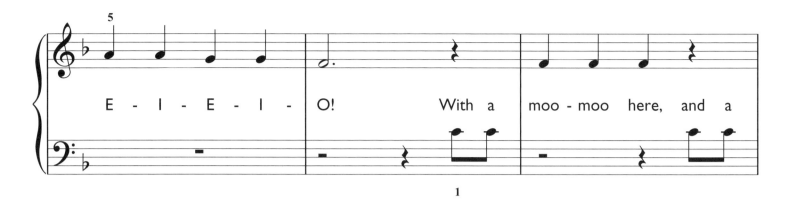

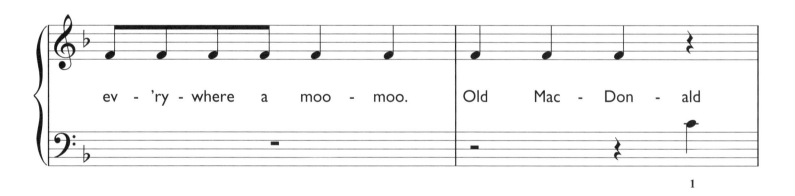

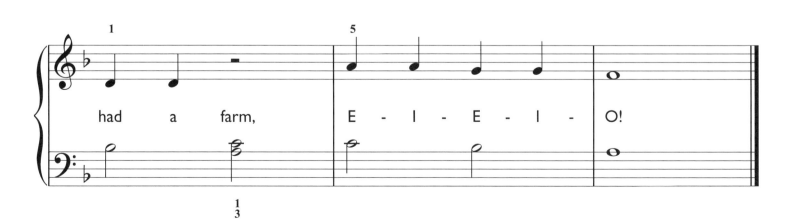

TO A WILD ROSE

Composed by Edward MacDowell

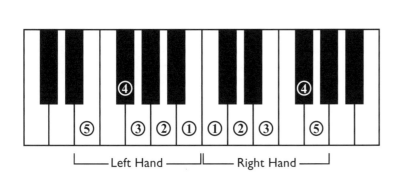

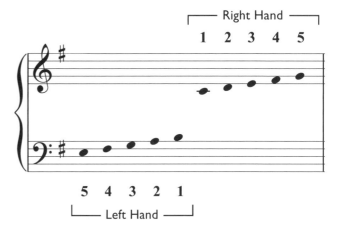

BARCAROLLE (from 'The Tales Of Hoffmann')

Composed by Jacques Offenbach

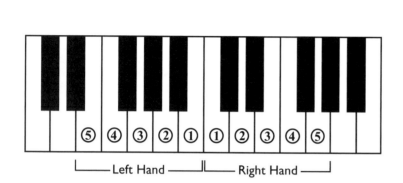

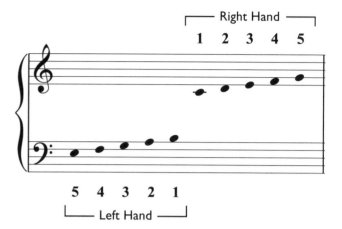

AVAILABLE IN THE
EASIEST 5-FINGER PIANO COLLECTION
SERIES...

Abba
A great collection of 15 classic Abba hits, including 'Dancing Queen', 'Fernando', 'Take A Chance On Me' and 'Thank You For The Music'.
AM998404

Ballads
A superb collection of 15 well-known ballads, including 'Fix You', 'I Have A Dream', 'Let It Be' and 'What A Wonderful World'.
AM995346

The Beatles
15 classic Beatles hits including 'All My Loving', 'Hey Jude', 'She Loves You' and 'Yellow Submarine'.
NO91322

New Chart Hits
15 top chart hits including 'Cry Me Out', 'Don't Stop Believin'', 'Issues', 'Just Dance' and 'Russian Roulette'.
AM1001077

Classical Favourites
15 classical pieces including 'Jupiter' (Holst), 'Lullaby' (Brahms), 'Minuet In G' (J.S. Bach) and 'Spring' (Vivaldi).
AM998393

Film Songs
15 great film songs including 'Breaking Free', 'Don't Worry, Be Happy', 'Somewhere Out There' and 'You've Got A Friend In Me'.
AM995335

Showtunes
15 great showtunes including 'Any Dream Will Do', 'Circle Of Life', 'Mamma Mia' and 'My Favourite Things'.
AM995324

Christmas
15 classic Christmas songs including 'Deck The Halls', 'Jingle Bells' and 'Walking In The Air' (Theme from 'The Snowman').
AM1001704

...PLUS MANY MORE

Published by
Wise Publications
14-15 Berners Street,
London W1T 3LJ, UK.

Exclusive Distributors:
Music Sales Limited
Distribution Centre, Newmarket Road,
Bury St Edmunds, Suffolk IP33 3YB, UK.
Music Sales Pty Limited
20 Resolution Drive, Caringbah,
NSW 2229, Australia.

Order No. AM1003112
ISBN 978-1-78038-014-8
This book © Copyright 2011 Wise Publications,
a division of Music Sales Limited.

Written by Christopher Hussey.
Edited by Lizzie Moore.

Printed in the EU.

Download to your computer a set of piano accompaniments for this *Piano Course* edition
(to be played by a teacher/parent).
Visit: **www.hybridpublications.com**
Registration is free and easy.
Your registration code is UG530

Your Guarantee of Quality
As publishers, we strive to produce every book to the highest commercial standards. This book has been carefully designed to minimise awkward page turns and to make playing from it a real pleasure. Particular care has been given to specifying acid-free, neutral-sized paper made from pulps which have not been elemental chlorine bleached. This pulp is from farmed sustainable forests and was produced with special regard for the environment. Throughout, the printing and binding have been planned to ensure a sturdy, attractive publication which should give years of enjoyment. If your copy fails to meet our high standards, please inform us and we will gladly replace it.